30 Day
Wisdom

Affirmational
Journal

INCREASE IN WISDOM WITH
30 DAYS OF WISDOM AFFIRMATIONS

Seyi Oshikanlu

30 Day Wisdom Affirmation Journal

Copyright@ Seyi Oshikanlu

First Edition September 2021

ISBN 978-1-7376334-0-2

Published and Distributed by Seyi Oshikanlu Ministries, Atlanta, Georgia USA

www.seyisohikanlu.org

For ordering information and or bulk purchase discounts please contact Seyi Oshikanlu Ministries by email at support@seyioshikanlu.org

Cover and Interior Design by JERA Publishing, Atlanta, Georgia USA

Contents

Preface

$\mathcal{T}$his journal is POWER-packed and will help you increase in wisdom and stand out from the pack in all spheres of life.

Wisdom is the application of knowledge or information, and Godly wisdom comes from God and can be explained as you having *'insider information'* and understanding and knowing things you actually know nothing about!

The word of God is medicine to our flesh (bodies).

"For they are life to those who find them, And health to all their flesh." Proverbs 4:22 NKJV

With this being the case, it is strongly suggested that you say these affirmations three times a day, as you would take prescribed medication.

Lastly, begin each day's affirmation session in a meditative mood as you start by thanking God for giving you His wisdom and honoring His word in your life.

What can you expect after 30 days?

The word of God is powerful and it delivers results all the time. As you consistently make these declarations or affirmations three times a day, you should expect that people will begin to gravitate towards you as a problem solver or a 'go-to' person, or a thought leader. You will find that you have clarity about situations and wise counsel will begin to flow out of you. You won't be confused and you won't be stumped in difficult circumstances.

In addition, expect comments such as "you are so wise.....I need to talk to you as you understand stuff' or even "you are the only one around here that gets it."

Whatever your experience please email us and let's hear your stories!

Get reading, thinking and writing!
To a wiser you!

Seyi Oshikanlu
www.seyioshikanlu.org

Wisdom Affirmational Journal

Day 1

*T*hank you, Lord, that I am taken captive by the words of my mouth.

I have the mind of Christ and I pay attention and acknowledge God's word and leading today. I do not succumb to peer pressure and I am never enticed to do evil. I consistently recognize all traps of the enemy and I simply step over these. Because I hear the voice of God, I can never be scammed or stolen from. I hear the voice of wisdom speaking to me every day and I stop in order to listen, therefore calamity doesn't befall me and things don't just happen to me, without my knowing.

Because I always have inside information, I regularly take opportunities and profit from these before others see them.

Today, I experience peace, I am free from fear and torment because I listen to God and I have the wisdom of God working for and through me right now.

Thank you, Lord!

What does having the mind of Christ mean to you?
1st Corinthians 2:16

_____

_____

_____

_____

_____

_____

_____

_____

_____

_____

_____

Day 2

hank you, Lord, that I have what I say.

I have searched out God's wisdom; therefore, I understand what God reveals to me and I am not confused about anything or anyone today. I clearly understand what I need to do and accomplish today and my day is not wasted. As a lover of God, I access God's storehouse of wisdom and I am abundantly supplied with wisdom. So I can now tackle all that life throws at me without cracking or having a melt or break down.

I am protected from evil and my paths do not cross with the immoral man or woman.

Today, I do and say the right things and I enjoy life to the fullest; free from blame and accusations.

I dwell in this city, and I am well rooted and I am prospering on every side.

Thank you, Lord!

How does my speech align with God's words? Mark 11:23

_____

_____

_____

_____

_____

_____

_____

_____

_____

_____

_____

_____

_____

Day 3

hank you, Lord, that today I receive the wisdom of God liberally. Today, I follow the instructions from the Word so my life is full and rewarding. I am faithful and loyal and I find favour in everything I do and everywhere I go. I trust the Lord completely and today I am guided by Him in every decision I make; hence, I make only wise choices. My accounts, businesses, and career keep growing and expanding upwards and I am in the overflow and I keep honoring God with this wealth.

I receive God's correction because I am a loved child of God. Today is a great day because I have found wisdom, long life, wealth, honour, and peace and they have all manifested!

As I wake up and lay down to sleep, I sleep soundly every day and God keeps me protected. Because of the wisdom of God I have, all my bills are paid on time. I enjoy excellent relationships with my family and neighbors, and as a friend of God, He gives me intimate secrets.

I walk under a constant stream of blessings as I enjoy grace and favour, and my legacy is honorable!

How do you receive God's counsel in your everyday life? Psalm 107:11

Day 4

*T*hank you, Lord, that my declarations today are spirit and life and I see results. Today, I was very attentive to the voice of the Holy Spirit, and I gained incredible insight into matters that concerned me today. I love wisdom and she keeps her eye on me and I do not make wrong turns in life or business and nor do I stumble or fumble around. Because I seek wisdom I am honored in my family, career, business, and community.

I do not engage in evil or wicked things but as one with right standing with God, things get progressively better for me daily and I burst with health. I guard my heart against evil, profanity, and uncleanness and life flows out of me to all I come in contact with. Today, I look ahead only, I watch my steps, I am not indecisive neither am I distracted. I receive all God has for me today.

In what ways does the Holy Spirit lead you? Do you see a trend? Romans 8:14

Day 5

Thank you, Lord, that today my ears and eyes are open to understanding, I have good sense and I always stay out of trouble. I am not deceived by the words of the seductive man or woman, and I do not get involved with him/her. Because I am wise, my life is not wasted or my resources squandered away. My life is prosperous and I build and leave a godly legacy to my descendants. I am not promiscuous and I delight in my partner alone. All that I do, all that I am doing is seen by the Lord and He is leading me daily. I am disciplined and I don't make foolish decisions that lead me astray. Today, my steps are ordered by the Lord.

In what ways do you avoid danger and life traps? Psalm 25:15

_____

_____

_____

_____

_____

_____

_____

_____

_____

_____

_____

_____

Day 6

*T*hank you, Lord, that today I actively avoid set traps. I am taken captive by my words. I do not stand as guarantors for friends or neighbors therefore I am not snared by circumstances beyond my control. My life is not at the mercy of any human being but only at God's mercy.

Like the ants, I make investments in fat times and I stockpile this every day for the day of harvest, therefore poverty never comes to me. My body is well-rested and I am never found napping or sleeping at the wrong times, therefore poverty is far from me. I do not tell lies, nor do I plot evil or is quick to do wrong. There is no strife in my family or environment because only the love of God manifests here. I receive wise counsel with ease and I have a teachable spirit.

My life is kept pure and I do not have relationships or affairs with another man or woman's partner. I do not lose my home, possession, or wealth due to infidelity. I am wise and I walk in wisdom daily.

What opportunities is God showing you? Ephesians 5:16

Day 7

hank you, Lord, that I treasure and pay attention to God's word today. Because I have common sense, I am never enticed by the flattery of the promiscuous man or woman. Today, I am at the right place at the right time and I am doing and getting the right results. I am not seduced into buying things I do not need, nor into getting into relationships I have no business being in because today I hear and yield to God's wisdom that speaks to me. So I never get in relationships or business transactions with the wrong people and I don't come up short!

My heart does not stray away towards evil and I am not a victim and nor am I a candidate for destruction. Today, I am kept safe and the Lord is pleased with me.

In what ways do you keep your focus on God? Jeremiah 29:13

_____

_____

_____

_____

_____

_____

_____

_____

_____

_____

_____

_____

_____

Day 8

*I*n this city I live, I literally hear and see wisdom speaking to me. In my industry, my business, my career, and my home, I respond, see, and understand situations and trends before they occur. This 'inside information' literally transforms me into a pacesetter and thought leader in my business and personal circumstances. Because of this, I consistently speak correctly as I understand what I am doing and what I need to do. When I communicate the insight I have to others, it comes across in a straightforward and understandable manner. Those that listen to me receive wisdom and knowledge that they deem as priceless and I am abundantly and even over-compensated for this.

God daily pours His wisdom into me, like water is poured into a container and as a result, I no longer have evil thoughts or desires nor am I prideful, and I don't speak with hate to anyone. Today, I understand and begin to experience a deeper walk with my God.

How did God give you wisdom recently? Proverbs 13:10

_____

_____

_____

_____

_____

_____

_____

_____

_____

_____

_____

_____

_____

_____

Day 9

*T*hank you, Lord, that as Your wisdom pours into me daily; I also hate what You hate, and I love what You love. I am able to receive counsel and sound knowledge which makes me a force to be reckoned with in all spheres of my life. The leadership decisions I make are just and fair, I keep rising in my leadership, and my success and prosperity attract positive attention, and yet God's love protects me. With the continuous and sustainable prosperity I am experiencing daily, I am building generational wealth and creating a legacy for others coming behind me as well. Thank you, Lord, that I am happy, playful, and I enjoy my family and friends, and I am not grumpy nor am I a complainer. I daily seek wisdom and I am obtaining more favor from God and man.

What does creating a legacy mean to you? Joshua 4.21-22

_____

_____

_____

_____

_____

_____

_____

_____

_____

_____

_____

_____

Day 10

Thank you, Lord, that my home, business, and career is built on Your wisdom. Today, wisdom is showing what I must do, in areas I lack clarity. The time I spend in meditation results in my knowing what to do and how to do this and I have crystal clear clarity daily. I do not engage with cynics, mockers, or angry people, and as such my life is not put in danger. Today, I instruct only those desiring to be instructed and they learn, understand, and become wiser. My time is not wasted on unproductive people or things but wisdom keeps extending my life and each day for me is more productive than the previous one. I mind my own business and I am not loud, noisy, or brash. My spirit is calm as I go about my day receiving insights from You. I am not deceived or led astray by foolish people and schemes, hence I am not deceived. Today, I enjoy the consequences of God's wisdom that operates in my life. Thank you, Lord!

How can you incorporate Bible meditation in your daily
routine? Joshua 1:8

_____

_____

_____

_____

_____

_____

_____

_____

_____

_____

Day 11

*T*hank you, Lord, that my life makes my parents happy as I have gained and continue to gain wealth honestly and consistently as directed by wisdom. Because I am not a slacker but I am diligent, I am not poor but my efforts always yield huge dividends. I recognize the season I am in and I do the right planning and planting now. I do not miss my moment, nor am I sleeping when my opportunity comes knocking, but I maximize my opportunities and I am enriched beyond human comprehension.

People that I relate to and deal with have good memories of their interactions with me and they are always blessed. I speak the truth only and peace follows me. The words I speak today are spirit and life. As a wise man/woman, I do not divulge all I know about situations and I learn all I need to know about a situation before I say only what is needed. I do not gossip or slander others as only foolish people do this and I am the wise. The words from my lips are like pure silver and my words carry value and worth. My words bless, help, and lift others up and I speak the mind of Christ.

What is the experience you want people to have of you consistently? Ephesians 5:1

_____

_____

_____

_____

_____

_____

_____

_____

_____

_____

_____

Day 12

hank you, Lord, that your blessings are what bring me wealth, and no hard work can add to this. I enjoy God's wisdom and I am getting what I want from God. I am not moved when trouble comes, because I already have the wisdom to navigate difficult situations. I am faithful and reliable and I get my jobs done. Today, I am in awe of God's love for me and I enjoy years of contented living and I am glad that I am seeing my dreams, hopes, and goals come to pass. God's strength is my strength and I am not cut down nor am I a barren tree and I am fruitful in all areas.

Thank you, Lord, that I deliver assignments with precision and accuracy, and I am dependable, faithful, and loyal.

How does the 'God Factor' impact your work? Proverbs 16:20

_____

_____

_____

_____

_____

_____

_____

_____

_____

_____

_____

_____

_____

Day 13

I am honest, I do not cheat or defraud people at work or at home and my business is aboveboard. I act as led by the spirit of God and not on presumptions or assumptions. I daily walk in humility and integrity making wise decisions that lead to good success and fulfillment. I am rich both in material substance and righteousness. Because I am honest, my path is straight and I am consistently delivered out of trouble that may arise in my life. As a good man/woman, my success at work and home is a blessing to many and my rising brings rejoicing in my spheres of influence. My neighbors and I are at peace and I speak well of them always and I keep quiet when needed. My city is safe and prosperous because I live there! My city is not ravaged by war, famine, or disease because the wisdom of God is manifest there.

I attract favor because I am kind and I keep experiencing the abundant life.

In what ways can you shine your light in your community? Matthew 5:14-16

_____

_____

_____

_____

_____

_____

_____

_____

_____

_____

_____

Day 14

I am not a borrower, but I lend to nations and I give generously. I give to strangers and I do not loan to them and suffer trouble, and I am not a servant to any lender. I do not guarantee debts or stand as surety to anyone as this is foolish and I am wise. The wicked gain deceptive wealth, but as the wise, I gain enduring generational wealth. The wicked will not go unpunished but those with right standing with God like me thrive like leafy trees. I am diligent and hence I prosper with no limitations to my possibilities and opportunities. I consistently learn from my mistakes and I won't repeat the same mistakes because I am wise. Thank you, Lord, for Your Word is working mightily in me.

Are there mistakes you tend to keep repeating? How can you address these? Proverbs 28:13-14

_____

_____

_____

_____

_____

_____

_____

_____

_____

_____

_____

Day 15

The words I speak bring me good success and I always think before I speak, so my life is protected and I do not come to financial, social, or physical ruin. I speak the truth always and I remain in right standing with God and He guards my way. There is no pretense in my life, and I am authentic and true to my values. My wealth is obtained by honest means and hence it does not dwindle but increases. My desires are fulfilled and I am always full of joy. Because I have the mind and intelligence of Christ, I win favor from others. My mind is flexible and I learn new things and therefore I do not display foolishness. Since I receive instruction and discipline easily, poverty and shame are far from me. I am prudent and I act with knowledge. As a good person, I leave an inheritance for my children's children and they are blessed to be related to me. Because I love my children, I am careful to discipline them and it is well with them. Thank you, Lord!

If you have the mind of Christ, can you trust your own thoughts? Philippians 2:5

_____

_____

_____

_____

_____

_____

_____

_____

_____

_____

Day 16

I build my house with wisdom and I do not use my own hands to tear it down but rather my home flourishes. As a wise person my lips protect me and I walk uprightly before the Lord. I have no deceit in me and I am not given to telling lies either. As I seek knowledge, I find this and this manifests in all I do. I do not go the way that seems right to me, but I go the way I am led by God to go. I am always rewarded for the good I do, and I consistently reap kindness. I am prudent and I give thought to all my actions and I am crowned with knowledge. My work brings profit and the wealth of the wise is their crown. My confidence is in God and He is my refuge and my safety. I have patience and this leads me to understand things thoroughly thus avoiding stupid mistakes and I am always the go-to person.

Thank you, Lord, that I have peace of mind, clarity of vision and I am fulfilling my purpose here on earth.

In what way do you reap what you sow? Galatians 6:7

_____

_____

_____

_____

_____

_____

_____

_____

_____

_____

_____

_____

Day 17

oday, my words are kind and I speak with wisdom and tact. I do not cause hurt or anger with my words and neither do I stir up strife. Wisdom flows out of me and my understanding increases daily. I seek out mentors, coaches, and counselors, and my life is propelling forward faster and I have a laser-beam focus on what I need to do daily. Thank you, Lord, that your ears are open to my prayers and everything with you is YES and Amen. The Lord knows and understands everything about me and I have a full assurance that He cares and is taking care of me. Nothing can separate me from His love. Because I have the right attitude and a cheerful heart; my life can be likened to a continual feast, and things are getting better every day for me. I am surrounded by your love and my life is moving forward like a super high way. I bring joy to my family and they are blessed to be associated with me.

How can you use your words to build up others?
1 Thessalonians 5:11

_____

_____

_____

_____

_____

_____

_____

_____

_____

_____

_____

Day 18

hank you, Lord, that I am not hot-tempered, and I do not fly off the handle today. I am calm, cool, and collected. Because I have an understanding of my circumstance, I am able to walk straight ahead into good success and with good advice, I am open to. The business and life I am building today get stronger every day and I don't get into pride. I am never greedy and I do not take bribes, hence I live long and well. Thank you, Lord, for Your goodness this day, this week, and this month. My plans are in your hands and I commit my work into your hands, Lord.

In what ways do your emotions affect your decision making? 2 Timothy 1:7

_____

_____

_____

_____

_____

_____

_____

_____

_____

_____

Day 19

oday, I walk in God's purpose for me, and I do not get off my own lane and I thank you, Lord, that confusion is far from me because I have clarity of mind and purpose. My ways please God and my enemies are at peace with me. I speak what is right and I delight those in authority over me and I am made known for your wisdom operating in my life. Today, my mind is clear, it receives downloads from God and I speak these truths as required. I do not dig up mischief nor do I sow strife. I am slow to anger and I have the rule over my spirit and hence, I keep growing and expanding, and all the events of my life are ordered by the Lord today.

How do you seek clarity from God consistently? Psalm 32:8

_____

_____

_____

_____

_____

_____

_____

_____

_____

_____

_____

_____

_____

_____

Day 20

hank you, Lord, for your wisdom in me and I do not cause shame to myself or my family. My heart and mind are not given to evil or wicked deeds nor am I a liar. Evil does not dwell in my house and I am not vindictive nor do I seek revenge on suffered loss. My life honours God, and I consistently help the poor and widowed. I forgive easily and I don't bear tales that destroy relationships. I am faithful and reliable and people can trust me in times of trouble. My heart is full of joy and gratitude for the great and awesome things God is doing daily, in me and through me. Today, I experience open doors, great favour, and unprecedented speed.

Are there people in your life you need to forgive?
If you do, what can you experience? Matthew 6:14-15

_____

_____

_____

_____

_____

_____

_____

_____

_____

_____

Day 21

*T*hank you, Lord, that I am not isolated from those You brought to surround me, and I do not seek any personal destructive desires. The words of my heart flow with wisdom and I don't enter into contention nor am I argumentative. I am committed to excellence and this attracts people and clients to me. I call on the name of the Lord and He always hears me, I recognize His voice and I am safe. When people speak to me, I listen attentively to the matter before I make a judgment and I am not a rash decision-maker. My heart is wise and I consistently acquire the right knowledge and information I need. Thank you, Lord, for gifts, talents, and passions because as I use these daily, I get better, and I am brought before great men because of these.

How can you build relationships with others in this season? Ephesians 4:16

_____

_____

_____

_____

_____

_____

_____

_____

_____

_____

_____

Day 22

hank you, Lord, I am satisfied by the fruit of my mouth. Death and life are in the power of my tongue and I speak life alone and not death. I speak to dead things, dead situations, dead businesses and they come back to life.

I have the favour of God over my life, I am friendly, and I attract true friends who stick closer than a brother to me. I maintain these relationships by integrity. I keep getting wiser every day and more good is attracted to me as a result of this. I am slow to anger and I ignore offenses. I am not a disaster to my family, business or community but rather a source of blessings, inspiration and hope. Thank you, Lord, that I increase on every side. My life is preserved and as I give to the poor, the Lord keeps giving back to me.

How can you intentionally grow in wisdom? 2 Peter 3:18

_____

_____

_____

_____

_____

_____

_____

_____

_____

_____

_____

Day 23

hank you, Lord, that my children are well disciplined, and I do not have issues with them. They listen to advice, accept instruction and we keep growing wiser as a family. The Lord's purpose for me succeeds and He causes my path to be clear to me. I honour my parents and my days are long on this earth. As an honorable person, I back off from needless fights as only fools jump right into these situations. I consistently do my work in the right seasons of life and hence I reap gigantic rewards. I am living my authentic self and I am known by my actions which honour God. People seek me out, as my speech is worth more than precious jewels. I do not gossip nor do I associate with those that talk too much. I don't make rash promises and when I do promise, I always deliver.

As a parent or mentor how do you want your life to speak to younger generations? 2 Timothy 2:2

_____

_____

_____

_____

_____

_____

_____

_____

_____

_____

Day 24

The Lord has access to all areas of my life, and as He searches me, I remain open to change and correction as needed. The Lord directs my heart to where He needs it to go so my plans end up in profit. I am systematic in my affairs and I don't rush needlessly around and end up in a loss. I am straight in my business dealings and my ways are pure. My home and business experience peace and trouble is far from me. I do not wander from the path of insight so I do not end up in dead situations, businesses or relationships. I have a guard over my mouth and I stay out of trouble. I am a giver and I keep getting a crazy harvest. Today, I experience victory, thank you, Lord!

What does focusing on Gods plan for your life look like for you? Psalm 91:14-15

_____

_____

_____

_____

_____

_____

_____

_____

_____

_____

_____

Day 25

hank you, Lord, that my reputation is honorable and it is priceless. I honour and respect all men because, like me, they are made by God. I remain humble before God and He rewards me with wealth, honour, and a good life. Because of the wisdom of God, I neither lend nor borrow money for consumer goods, and I am not a slave to the lender. My speech is gracious and I attract the attention of kings and industry leaders. I consistently support the poor or less privileged as I can and hence I lend to the Lord this way. All my needs are met and my bills are paid and I have plenty more to put in the store.

How can you expand your network by moving out of your comfort zone or community? Colossians 3:12-14

_____

_____

_____

_____

_____

_____

_____

_____

_____

_____

_____

Day 26

hank you, Lord, because I have a pure heart and thus I speak with grace, and kings are attracted to me as friends. Wisdom is on the tip of my tongue, and I always speak the right words at the right time. I speak only the truth and I give accurate reports as required in my life endeavors.

I live in harmony with my neighbors and I do not trample on anyone's rights or privileges. I do not guarantee loans for others and I am not a borrower either. I am extremely efficient in my work, I am good at spotting and consistently get great opportunities that launch my life and career into higher levels with ease.

What does authentic living mean to you and how can you pursue this? Romans 12:1-21

_____

_____

_____

_____

_____

_____

_____

_____

_____

_____

_____

Day 27

hank you, Lord, that I am not greedy nor is my appetite for anything out of control. I do not experience burnout and I know when to rest and take breaks as required. I am a generous soul and I enjoy pleasant conversations with guests, family, and friends. My children are disciplined, well trained, and taught of God. I fear the Lord consistently and my hope and future are secure in Him. The wisdom of God keeps my mind going in the right direction and I consistently get more wisdom, discipline, and understanding.

What ways can you pursue rest? 2 Corinthians 4:16

_____

_____

_____

_____

_____

_____

_____

_____

_____

_____

_____

_____

Day 28

*T*hank you, Lord, that my mind does not think up or plot evil. My family, business, and career is built with understanding and these are established on Godly principles. All areas of my life experience abundance and unusual favor. I am strategic in all my dealings and I operate fully in my zone of genius. I regularly receive divine downloads which sets me apart from my competitors and causes me to have strength in uncertain times. Because life happens for me and not to me, every circumstance and situation is working out for my good. Thank you, Lord, that in all situations and at all times, I give you the glory.

When did you experience the help of God in turning things around for you? Can you trust Him to do this again? Isaiah 40:31

_____

_____

_____

_____

_____

_____

_____

_____

_____

_____

_____

Day 29

oday, the Lord makes all matters plain to me. I know what I need to do and say today, and I am not confused. I receive inside information regarding any contentious matter and things work out without long legal battles. I say the right words at the right time and I am open to correction. Because I am friendly, I have good friends and I am not a bother but I am a blessing to my family and friends. I am sensitive to the needs of both my friends and family and the Lord rewards me for this. I exhibit a high level of self-control and emotional intelligence. Thank you, Lord, that I represent you well here on earth.

Do you feel you are going in God's direction for your life? What can you do to make this happen, if need be? Proverbs 3:5-6

_____

_____

_____

_____

_____

_____

_____

_____

_____

_____

Day 30

hank you, Lord, that I am immune to curses and spells as I am covered by the blood of Jesus. I don't speak as a fool neither do I hire fools or those not properly vetted, as wisdom guides my decision making. As a wise person, I can see trouble coming and I avoid this. My friends are people of substance and we constantly sharpen each other.

Whatever is committed to me prospers and I grow in my work exponentially and I am mindful of what my hand finds to do. I do not suffer lack or want as the Lord meets my every need.

How does the blood of Jesus protect YOU? Ephesians 1:7

_____

_____

_____

_____

_____

_____

_____

_____

_____

_____

_____

_____

_____

Bonus Day
Day 31

*T*hank you, Lord, that I am as bold as a lion. I obey the law of the land and I oppose evil and wrongdoing. I am led by God, and His ears are open to my prayers always and I daily accept and receive good things and pleasant surprises. I respect all human beings, and so I am blessed. I am not involved in get-rich quick schemes, and I have no desire or tendency towards these schemes. I am a global influencer and my wisdom is sought after in my industry. I rely on God, and He guides and leads me into all I need to know and do and so I abound in blessings. Thank you, Lord, for the opportunities I have to keep giving to the poor. Your word is a shield to me. I am a wise man or woman and I get wiser every day!

How can you increase your confidence in God? 1 John 5:14

_____

_____

_____

_____

_____

_____

_____

_____

_____

_____

_____

About the Author

Seyi Oshikanlu is an author, Bible teacher, conference speaker and transformational life coach. Seyi started her public life, as a youth college pastor and now leads a ministry that helps women overcome fear, gain clarity and step into their divine purpose with confidence before they run out of time.

She ministers under a prophetic anointing and is gifted by God to call out your greatness!

As a Christian business woman, she has created online courses and teaches how to gain life clarity and live life by design. She regularly facilitates faith based masterminds, and group coaching sessions. Seyi, also teaches praying for results and shows people how to think correctly and get the right results. She is married and lives with her husband and two children in the USA.

For more information please visit www.seyioshikanlu.org

Made in the USA
Columbia, SC
13 February 2025

53753091R00045